BIRDER

Julie Marie Myatt

BROADWAY PLAY PUBLISHING INC
New York
www.broadwayplaypublishing.com
info@broadwayplaypublishing.com

Cover photo by Julie Marie Myatt

First edition: November 2019
I S B N: 978-0-88145-812-1

Book design: Marie Donovan
Page make-up: Adobe InDesign
Typeface: Palatino

BIRDER was commissioned by Center Theatre Group, Los Angeles.

BIRDER was first produced by the Road Theatre (produced by Donna Simone Johnson and Ann Hearn) in North Hollywood running from 25 April-19 June 2016. The cast and creative contributors were:

ROGER... Chet Grissom
JOYCE .... Laurie Okin
CHARLES.. Webster Williams
REBECCA .... Monique Marie Gelineau
TODD.. Crash Buist

Director ....Dan Bonnell
Set design ....Tom Buderwitz
Lighting & projection design .... Tom Ontiveros
Sound design...David Marling
Costume design ....Michele Young
Stage manager... Maurie Gonzalez

CHARACTERS & SETTING

ROGER
JOYCE
REBECCA
CHARLES
TODD

Cast should reflect the diversity of the population in California

Los Angeles
Time: The Great Recession

"Life is getting more complicated, but it seems the more artificially complex man's affairs become, the more he yearns for the fundamentals, the things of earth…the boom in birding, seems to be an antidote to the pressures and artificialities of the modern world."
Roger Tory Peterson, 1948

For Dan Bonnell, with love and appreciation

ACT ONE

(The sound of Los Angeles–area birds as audience enters the theatre.)

Scene 1

(Sound of birds continues. Morning light)

(The present)

(ROGER enters in his pajamas, carrying a cup of coffee, listening. He wears glasses.)

ROGER: You hear that?

(ROGER points to the sound of the birds, smiling.)

ROGER: Hear that? *That.*

(He listens. Points)

That's a house finch. *Carpodacus mexicanus.* You'd recognize it. Not a flashy looking bird, but we have a lot of them in L A. The males have an orange or red head and chest.

(Silence)

I used to live up in Los Feliz. Right up from what used to be the Brown Derby. (It's now a brightly lit Chase Bank.) A couple of house finch built a nest up in the eves on my back porch. Right outside my back door. (It was a nice 1920s Spanish style, the house) I got a perfect view of the nest if I stood on a kitchen chair and stared through the window. I was riveted…Mother and father bird working together…I stood there for hours waiting for the chicks to hatch, and later, waiting for the parents to return with food when they did…. One day I watched the father carefully feeding the chicks, and it basically destroyed my sense of myself. Who I was. What I was doing with my life. He turned to look me in the eye, and I swear that bird saw right through me, right to my gut, and I cried like a baby. I stood on that chair and cried. You know why? That bird saw me. *Me*. He saw the truth. He knew he had his shit together, and I didn't. He was a man, taking care of his family, feeding his kids, doing whatever he had to do, fighting the bird racket, sucking it up. And what the hell was I doing? Standing on chairs? … Crying like a baby? He took me down with one quick bird-eyed glance… Cocksucker… Oh, I hated that bird. Who the hell did he think he was? What did he know about mortgages? Debt. College funds. Sports camps. Breast implants. *My* house did not grow on trees and come from hair and dryer lint like his. No… What an asshole…that freeloading house finch. I—

JOYCE: *(O S)* Honey?

ROGER: Yes.

(A woman brings a coffee pot on stage. JOYCE. *She's* ROGER's *wife. Mid-forties. Dressed nicely for work. Smiling)*

JOYCE: More coffee?

ROGER: Oh. Yes. Please.

*(*JOYCE *refills* ROGER's *coffee cup. Looking at his pajamas)*

ROGER: Thank you. Tastes good.

JOYCE: Breakfast will be ready in ten minutes.

ROGER: Thanks, honey.

*(*JOYCE *looks at* ROGER's *pajamas again.)*

JOYCE: You're, you're going to work today, right?

ROGER: Yes.

(JOYCE *begins to exit.*)

ROGER: Why?

JOYCE: I'll be at work late tonight, and I want the kids to know what to expect.

ROGER: I'll pick them up at three-thirty.

JOYCE: That's what I'll tell them.

ROGER: Good.

JOYCE: And you'll make dinner?

ROGER: Of course.

JOYCE: Wonderful. Thank you.
(*She smiles and exits.*)

ROGER: Where was I?

(ROGER *looks at the audience, about to say something, then another bird sound O S.*)

ROGER: Hear that! Common Raven! *Corvus corax.* Most people have little interest in ravens. I love them. They're very very smart, you know. The majority of the time, if not all of the time, people mistake ravens for just your ordinary crow or blackbird.
(*He looks up toward the bird. Starts to sing Beatles song,* Blackbird.)
"Blackbird singing in the dead of night…take these broken wings and learn to fly—"

JOYCE: (*O S*) Roger?

ROGER: What?

JOYCE: (*O S*) You're, you're getting ready for work, right?

ROGER: Yes. I just told you I was.

JOYCE: *(O S)* It sounds like you're singing.

ROGER: I can sing and dress, Joyce!
(Silence)
Where was I? What was I…
(He thinks.)
Oh. Right. There is one thing that I think that house finch—

JOYCE: *(O S)* Roger?

ROGER: What?

JOYCE: *(O S)* Are you really—

ROGER: Yes!

JOYCE: *(O S)* It's just that, it's, it's kind of getting late, honey, and if you want to shower and shave—

ROGER: I'm getting ready, Joyce!
(He starts to say more—)

JOYCE: *(O S)* I'm really not trying to nag, sweetheart! I'm just being supportive! Lots of support here!

ROGER: Thank you, honey!
(He begins to speak again—)

JOYCE: *(O S)* It's just, just that I don't want everyone to get a late start again today. I've got a big day at work. I'm really hoping to close that deal.

(ROGER starts to speak again—)

JOYCE: *(O S)* We could use the money. Right?

(Silence)

(More silence)

JOYCE: *(O S)* Roger?

(ROGER swallows more coffee, looking at the audience, and exits.)

Scene 2

(Slide: Two years ago. Griffith Park)

(A thirty-something outdoorsy woman enters quietly, REBECCA, *then an older man in his sixties,* CHARLES, *then finally,* ROGER. ROGER *wears a different pair of glasses. They all carry binoculars and cameras.* ROGER *moves in close beside* REBECCA.*)*

*(*CHARLES *is listening carefully. He moves slowly, encouraging* ROGER *and* REBECCA *to do the same, and listen.)*

ROGER: You look beautiful.

CHARLES: Sshh…please.

(They continue to walk quietly.)

ROGER: I like your—

CHARLES: Sshh….

ROGER: *(Quieter)* I like your hat.

CHARLES: Sshh.

(Silence)

*(*CHARLES *stops, listens.)*

ROGER: *(Quieter)* Where, where did you get it?

CHARLES: Sshh.

(Silence)

REBECCA: *(Whispering)* I ordered it.

ROGER: Wow. Where?

CHARLES: Sshh.

REBECCA: *(Whispering)* On line.

CHARLES: Sshh.

ROGER: *(Quieter)* Really? Wow—

REBECCA: It was on sale.

ROGER: It's, it's very becoming.

CHARLES: Sshh.

(He listens. Points his binoculars to a tree)

*(*REBECCA *follows* CHARLES' *lead.)*

ROGER: I like—

CHARLES: Are you here to flirt or watch birds?

ROGER: I can't comment on Rebecca's lovely—

CHARLES: No.

(Very long silence)

(A bird sound O S)

*(*REBECCA *smiles at* CHARLES.*)*

*(*ROGER *looks to the trees.)*

*(*CHARLES *points to a far off tree. Binoculars to eyes)*

(Everyone silently looks. The bird flies off.)

CHARLES: Purple finch.

REBECCA: Wow.

CHARLES: First one this year.

REBECCA: Beautiful.

CHARLES: The colors were so vibrant.

REBECCA: Incredible.

CHARLES: Just wonderful.

ROGER: Missed it.

*(*CHARLES *takes a small note pad from his pocket, and adds purple finch to his on-going list.)*

CHARLES: You're not looking.

ROGER: I am too.

CHARLES: Not at the right bird.

(CHARLES *watches as* ROGER *unfolds a portable camping stool, takes out a thermos of coffee and some doughnuts. Makes himself a little picnic. Offers it to the others*)

CHARLES: Roger.

REBECCA: No, no thank you.

CHARLES: Why didn't you eat breakfast before you came? I've told you—

ROGER: I didn't have time.

CHARLES: Why not?

ROGER: I had to drop the kids off at soccer.

CHARLES: So early?

ROGER: They're state champions. They start early.
(*Silence*)
You should come watch them some time. They really are quite good. For their age, of course. I mean—

CHARLES: You are really testing my patience.

ROGER: Why?

CHARLES: I thought you were interested in birding—

ROGER: I am.

CHARLES: You said in your post you were looking for a mentor in the "bird world" and—

ROGER: I am—

CHARLES: Then let me mentor! Let me do my job! Put the food away and stop—

ROGER: I'm hungry. And is it my fault you have a beautiful daughter?

CHARLES: Who will stop joining us, if you don't behave. I won't be the man who helps ruin a marriage.

ROGER: Keep your shorts on. My marriage is fine. Please. It's all in good fun.

(He winks at REBECCA.*)*
Right?

CHARLES: Is it fun for you Rebecca? This blatant display—

REBECCA: I don't care. I'm flattered.

CHARLES: Rebecca. Please.

REBECCA: What?

CHARLES: It's obnoxious. And undignified. Save it for the bar. Both of you.

ROGER: I don't go to bars.

REBECCA: Me either.

CHARLES: Maybe you should.
(Silence)
You sure you *really* want to learn about birds, Roger?

ROGER: Yes.

CHARLES: Why?

ROGER: I had a, a personal experience. With a house finch.

CHARLES: And?

REBECCA: Uh, obviously, Dad takes this very seriously—

ROGER: I want to know what it means. And—

CHARLES: What it means?

ROGER: I've been living in this city for twenty years, and I am just now noticing there are *birds* among us here, I mean really noticing? What else might I be missing? I've obviously been living blindly.
(Silence)
Very very blindly.
(Silence)
I may have missed my entire life.

CHARLES: There are professionals available. For these kinds of questions. With couches and PhDs.

ROGER: You have a PhD.

CHARLES: In biology. Not psychology.

ROGER: I don't need therapy. Thank you.

CHARLES: Why not?

ROGER: I've tried it. It did not take.

CHARLES: Uh huh.

(REBECCA checks her phone.)

ROGER: Is that a text?

(REBECCA smiles.)

ROGER: Who, who is the text from?

CHARLES: What kind of work do you do again?

(ROGER is busy trying to look at REBECCA's phone.)

CHARLES: Roger?

ROGER: What?

CHARLES: What kind of work do you do? I've forgotten.

ROGER: I'm an accountant.

CHARLES: That's right. For a major law firm, yes?

ROGER: Uh huh.

CHARLES: With big clients?

ROGER: Yeah.

CHARLES: You really want to know what you've been missing there?

(Silence)

ROGER: What are you saying?

CHARLES: You know one of the reasons people love birding so much?

ROGER: Birds are interesting.

CHARLES: Nope. Sorry. Wrong answer. Find another mentor.

REBECCA: Dad.

ROGER: C'mon.

CHARLES: People love to get out here, *in the quiet*, and watch birds to get away from the rest of their lives. To see something else, not what they have to see at home, or in their domestic or career lives. *In the peace and quiet.* This world is full of surprises, full of anticipation and wonder—one of the last vestiges of true wonder. And one of the last vestiges of listening, true, careful listening, to the *quiet* noise of nature. It is pure and unsoiled by the rattle of human minds, greed and corruption, removed from the bullshit of corporations, technology, and law firms. Rebecca, put that phone away.

REBECCA: Dad—

CHARLES: Do it. You know the rules.

ROGER: What are you trying to say?

CHARLES: Birding will not fix your mid-life crisis.

ROGER: How do you know?

CHARLES: It might ease the burden, but it will not fix it.

ROGER: How do you know?

(Silence)

REBECCA: Dad.

(Silence)

ROGER: I didn't say it would…fix it.

CHARLES: Really?

ROGER: And I'm not in a mid-life crisis. Please. I'm not a cliché, thank you very much. I'm simply looking for a new hobby. Time in nature. Peace. "Wonder." Is that a crime?

CHARLES: No. But this is for the serious-minded.

ROGER: What part of me is not "serious-minded"?

CHARLES: Your mind.

ROGER: That's not fair.

CHARLES: I've taken you out on two trips and so far you have tried to ask Rebecca to lunch, four times, tried to leave your trash in the woods, arguing that wax paper and aluminum were *essentially* "biodegradable", you made phone calls during five critical sighting moments, and you have yet to arrive in a timely manner, making us wait at least fifteen to twenty minutes for your arrival, and when you do arrive, you are still not ready…shaving as you get out of the car, brushing your teeth, and paying bills on your iphone…ectera…

ROGER: I wasn't paying bills—

CHARLES: If you want or need a hobby, why don't you take up softball or stamp collecting. Maybe cartography.

ROGER: Why did you answer my ad?

CHARLES: Why not join a group? Audubon is perfect for you.

ROGER: I'm not a joiner. Why did you answer my ad?

CHARLES: I enjoy sharing the birding experience with others.

ROGER: Exactly—

CHARLES: But not you.

ROGER: I could be your greatest student.

CHARLES: And ruin my every quiet experience?

ROGER: Or enhance. I could enhance. Obviously you are looking for new kinds of companionship.

CHARLES: How is that obvious?

ROGER: Craigslist.
(Silence)
That's got lonely written all over it. You are lonely, Charles. Admit it.

REBECCA: *(Softly)* Okay, Roger…

CHARLES: I may be…a bit…a bit…lonely…since my wife died and Rebecca thinks I need to make more effort to, to meet people so I did what she told me. Right, you told me to go on Craigslist. You said it might expand my friends beyond my immediate circle of birders—

REBECCA: I did.

CHARLES: I thought I'd *try*. No hurt in *trying*. I can't spend my life mourning my wife. And Rebecca is trying to help me. I know that. Even coming on these trips is a way of her making sure that I meet good, solid companions, not crazy Craiglist people. I am well aware of that.

REBECCA: Dad—

ROGER: So why give up on me so easy?

CHARLES: You're a pain in the ass. I'd rather be alone.

ROGER: Look, Charles.
(He pours himself another cup of coffee.)
It seems to me you and I have some things in common.

CHARLES: No we don't. We have nothing in common.

ROGER: You are clearly not a joiner.

REBECCA: He hates groups.

ROGER: And you need a friend who you can teach things to, who you can feel superior to—

CHARLES: That's not true—

REBECCA: It is a little, Dad—

ROGER: And I need to find something of meaning in my life.

CHARLES: You have a wife and two kids. You have—

ROGER: It's not enough.

CHARLES: Then you aren't trying very hard.

ROGER: Was it enough for you?

CHARLES: That's not the point.

REBECCA: Dad.

CHARLES: You can't compare your life to mine.

ROGER: Why not?

CHARLES: You just can't.

REBECCA: Dad got out of the house as much as possible.

CHARLES: Not true.

REBECCA: You went birding every weekend.

CHARLES: You came with me.

REBECCA: Only when mom wasn't home and you couldn't get a baby sitter.

CHARLES: That's not true.

REBECCA: *(To* ROGER*)* It's true.

ROGER: See? We have a lot in common, Charles. You could learn a lot from me too.

CHARLES: What? Name one thing.
(Silence)
One thing.
(Silence)

ROGER: Well. We shall see, won't we? We shall see. I could be *your* mentor. In some way. In some capacity.

CHARLES: What capacity?

ROGER: Companionship. Right, Rebecca?

REBECCA: Right.

CHARLES: I'd rather get a dog.

ROGER: I'm way more fun than a dog.

(CHARLES *just looks at* ROGER.)

CHARLES: Don't be so sure.

(CHARLES *exits.* REBECCA *smiles meekly, and follows.*)

(ROGER *quickly follows.*)

Scene 3

(*Living room*)

(ROGER *and* JOYCE's *lovely living room in their very tasteful Los Feliz home. She folds laundry. She is very exacting about her folding.*)

(*Each child's shirt she takes a long time getting each crease right.*)

(ROGER *enters in suit and tie.*)

JOYCE: Good day at work?

ROGER: Sure. Great.

JOYCE: The kids are at Andy's house. He's got some new video game they want.

ROGER: Uh huh.

JOYCE: I told them they would have to wait until Christmas or Chanukah. Ask Santa.

ROGER: Is it expensive?

JOYCE: I don't know.
(*Silence*)
Are you hungry?

ROGER: No. Not terribly—

JOYCE: Because I haven't started dinner.

ROGER: That's okay. I can wait.

(Silence)

JOYCE: We could…you know…

ROGER: What?

JOYCE: You know…

ROGER: What?

JOYCE: You know…

(Silence)

ROGER: Sex?

JOYCE: Uh huh.

ROGER: Now?

JOYCE: Yes.

ROGER: I'm tired.

JOYCE: Really?

ROGER: Yes—

JOYCE: But the house is all ours—

ROGER: The law firm has a big new corporate account, which I cannot name, that is basically a mess—

JOYCE: It was just a suggestion.
(She continues folding.)

ROGER: And one I really appreciate. Really. Honest.
(He takes off his jacket.)

JOYCE: Okay.

ROGER: I'm sorry.

JOYCE: I get it.

ROGER: I'm still looking at numbers. In my head. It's all numbers and—

JOYCE: I get it.

ROGER: You know how it is.

JOYCE: Not really, but I will try.

ROGER: Well, if you were working, you would. It's not so easy to turn on and off. When you come home.

JOYCE: Roger.

ROGER: What?

JOYCE: I used to work, very hard, and I still wanted to come home and have sex with you.

ROGER: You're an athlete, Joyce.

JOYCE: What's that got to do with anything?

ROGER: Your stamina is very high.

JOYCE: Uh huh.

ROGER: You gave birth to our kids like you were hiking a football.

JOYCE: Roger.

ROGER: It's true. Even the nurses were amazed.

JOYCE: Roger.

ROGER: What?

JOYCE: That's not funny.

ROGER: I think it is—

JOYCE: Never mind.

ROGER: What?

JOYCE: Never mind.

ROGER: What?

(Silence)

JOYCE: I need you to be more romantic.

ROGER: I am romantic. I'm the most romantic guy around. I'm just tired today.

JOYCE: Okay. Okay. But let it just be known.

ROGER: What?

JOYCE: I am missing some…

ROGER: Some…?

JOYCE: Passion.

ROGER: I give you passion.

JOYCE: Well—

ROGER: I give you passion.

JOYCE: You do?

ROGER: Yes.

JOYCE: When?

ROGER: All the time.

JOYCE: Then I want more.

ROGER: I bought you the breast implants.

JOYCE: What's that got to—

ROGER: You wanted them. Not me. I thought your boobs were terrific. I liked your boobs, just how they were.

JOYCE: It's not about my boobs.

ROGER: I like them now too, of course—

JOYCE: That's not the point.

ROGER: What's the point?

JOYCE: You don't make me feel sexy.

ROGER: You are sexy.

JOYCE: I don't feel it.

ROGER: Is that my fault?

JOYCE: Yes.

ROGER: How?

JOYCE: I am home all day with the kids—

ROGER: Not all day. They have school—

JOYCE: Most of the day, and I need, I really need, when you come home, for you to *see* me. Really *see* me.

ROGER: I see you.

JOYCE: I mean, I'm not proud that I feel this way, but I do—

ROGER: I see you.

JOYCE: It doesn't feel like it.

ROGER: I am under a lot of pressure.

JOYCE: Wouldn't sex relieve the pressure?

ROGER: Joyce—

JOYCE: Seriously.

ROGER: It doesn't always work that way.

JOYCE: Well, it makes me feel ugly and rejected and than I feel stupid for feeling that way. I feel stupid and needy and pathetic.

ROGER: You're beautiful. (And pathetic.)

JOYCE: Not funny.

(ROGER *puts his arms around* JOYCE.)

ROGER: I'm sorry. You are beautiful. (And needy.)

JOYCE: Roger.

(ROGER *kisses* JOYCE.)

ROGER: I love you.
(*He kisses her again.*)
You are so sexy.

(ROGER *kisses* JOYCE *again and pulls her closer.*)

JOYCE: You smell like cigarette smoke.

ROGER: Do I?

JOYCE: Uh huh.

ROGER: Must be from one of the lawyers at work. I was standing outside talking to him.
(He kisses her more and rubs his hands along her body.)
Let's go to the bedroom.

JOYCE: Wow. Roger. You smell, you smell like an ashtray.

ROGER: I do not.

JOYCE: You do. Were you smoking?

ROGER: Please.

(JOYCE pulls away.)

JOYCE: Just take a quick shower and wash your hair and meet me in bed. It'll take two seconds.

(ROGER lets out a loud groan.)

ROGER: Joyce.

JOYCE: What?

ROGER: Do you know how tired I am?

JOYCE: A shower will refresh you.

ROGER: Do you know how much energy a shower takes? All that scrubbing. And rinsing. And drying—

JOYCE: Don't be lazy, Roger. C'mon. Meet me in bed.
(She kisses him, grabs the folded clothes and exits.)

(ROGER watches her exit, then slumps on the couch. He slowly pulls off his tie.)

(He stares at the walls around him. His nice house)

(He unbuttons his shirt.)

(He smells the sleeve.)

JOYCE: *(O S)* Roger?

ROGER: Coming!

JOYCE: *(O S)* Oh, grab some wine, sweetheart! Let's make this special, Okay? Get a good bottle!

(ROGER slowly gets up.)

ROGER: Okay.

JOYCE: *(O S)* What, honey?

ROGER: I said, okay!

JOYCE: *(O S)* And don't forget the glasses. You don't want to make two trips. Right?

(ROGER takes out a pack of cigarettes and a lighter and opens a window. He stands smoking in a corner of the stage.)

(He looks at the cigarette, takes a deep drag and puts it out.)

(An owl hoots O S.)

ROGER: Great Horned Owl. Calling for his mate.

(The owl hoots again O S.)

(ROGER smiles.)

ROGER: They have it so easy. Life among the tall tree tops. The night air.

JOYCE: *(O S)* Roger?

ROGER: What freedom.

(The owl hoots again O S.)

ROGER: Real freedom.
(He exits.)

Scene 4

(Outside)

(CHARLES enters with binoculars to the trees. ROGER follows, binoculars to the ground.)

ROGER: Charles?

CHARLES: Sshh.

ROGER: *(Softer)* Charles?

CHARLES: Sshh.

ROGER: Did Rebecca have a date today?

CHARLES: None of your business.

ROGER: An appointment?

CHARLES: Sssh.

ROGER: *(Softer)* Is she okay?

CHARLES: She's fine.
(He listens.)
(Sound of a hawk O S)
(CHARLES points.)

ROGER: What?

CHARLES: There.

ROGER: What?

CHARLES: Cooper's Hawk.

(ROGER points his binoculars.)

ROGER: Nice. Very nice.

CHARLES: Nothing so uncommon, but still beautiful. Huh?

ROGER: Yes.

CHARLES: Majestic. Proud.

ROGER: Very.

CHARLES: Wonderful.

ROGER: Did you see it look at me?

CHARLES: No.

ROGER: So why didn't she come?

CHARLES: Who?

ROGER: Rebecca.

CHARLES: I asked her not to.

ROGER: Because...

CHARLES: I don't need a baby sitter. And you don't need a distraction.

ROGER: But she's so nice. And cute.

CHARLES: (Jesus.)
(He takes his note pad out of his pocket and adds the Coopers Hawk.)

ROGER: Don't get all bent out of shape. I just enjoy her company. And the smell of her hair. I'm not trying to get in her pants, if that's what you're afraid of.

CHARLES: I am.

ROGER: I've got a lot of pressure in my life right now, a lot, and a little extra beauty, a nice smile, and fresh smelling shampoo is a small bit of welcome pleasure. That's all.

CHARLES: Smell the fresh air.

ROGER: I'm trying.
(He is beginning to get upset.)

CHARLES: Listen to the sound of the birds. That's what we're here for.

ROGER: I'm trying.

CHARLES: Look at the sky. The trees.

ROGER: I can't see the forest for the trees, Charles.

CHARLES: What?

ROGER: I can't... *(He puts his head in his hands and cries.)*

CHARLES: (Oh dear.)

ROGER: I'm sorry. I just...

(CHARLES *hands* ROGER *a handkerchief from his pocket.*)

(ROGER *blows his nose.*)

ROGER: Thank you.
(*He wipes his eyes.*)

ROGER: I just…I just don't know what to do.

CHARLES: About what?

ROGER: My life.

CHARLES: What about it? Is it your marriage?

ROGER: No. Not my marriage. I love Joyce. I do…
We're fine. It's my life. Everything else. But maybe that
relates. I guess my marriage relates too. I don't know.
Hell.
(*He blows his nose again. Unfolds his camp chair and sits
down.*)

CHARLES: What's the issue?

ROGER: Money.

CHARLES: I see.

ROGER: Money…
(*He starts to cry again.*)
I'm sorry. I'm sorry. I've been crying a lot lately.

CHARLES: No problem.

ROGER: Not in public, of course.

CHARLES: Of course.

ROGER: I just…I don't know, I just don't ever seem
to have enough money. There's just not enough. No
matter how hard I try, there is never enough money to
go around. The pressure is unbearable.

CHARLES: You have a good job.

ROGER: Yes. Well…

CHARLES: So what's the problem?

ROGER: My life is just too fucking expensive. I can't keep up. I can't…I'm an accountant, for Christ's sake. I should know. I can't make it add up.

CHARLES: Right.

ROGER: And Joyce wants things for the boys and I feel like I'm being a bad father if I say no. And she wants things for herself, and I want her to be happy, so I don't want to stop her from getting what she wants, but there's just not enough money to do it all and I have mortgaged the house twice and there's private school for two kids, and now Joyce wants to take the kids to Disneyworld next summer and I want to say, what the hell, we live near Disney*land*, but I guess there is some big difference…I don't know what it is, but there is a difference, I guess—

CHARLES: Florida.

ROGER: I guess.

CHARLES: Epcot Center. They have Epcot Center.

ROGER: Yeah. That's what Joyce says.
(He blows his nose.)
But it will cost thousands of dollars and I am beyond maxed out, beyond, and if I make a big deal of it, I look like I'm cheap or a bad father or I don't want to give the boys everything boys should have. Or need. Or that they're friends have.

CHARLES: They will be fine without Disneyworld. And Epcot Center. Trust me.

ROGER: You've been?

(Silence)

CHARLES: I took Rebecca there.
(Silence)
Things were cheaper back then.

ROGER: Uh huh.

CHARLES: They were different times.

ROGER: Maybe.

CHARLES: She was an only child.

ROGER: My parents didn't take me to do all that stuff
and I turned out all right.
(Silence)
I mean, we had to play in the yard. And in the
neighborhood. That's it. My dad never took us
anywhere. He was too busy working. We just had to go
in the back yard and *imagine* things…there wasn't all
this competition about who had what and who went
where, because none of us went anywhere. Maybe to
the beach. Maybe to New York City to see the Statue of
Liberty. Once. Maybe to the mall to play video games.
And I think one kid went to Disneyland in fourth
grade, but only because his dad won the trip from a
cereal box. But other than that, life was pretty basic.
For everyone.

CHARLES: Where'd you grow up?

ROGER: New York.

CHARLES: City?

ROGER: No. Jamestown.

CHARLES: No kidding. Big birding community there.

ROGER: Why?

CHARLES: Roger Tory Peterson is from there.

ROGER: Who's he?

CHARLES: One of the founders of birding in America.

ROGER: Come to think of it, I guess me and my friends
used to shoot robins with our bb guns.

CHARLES: Uh huh.

ROGER: I had big plans to travel the world then.

CHARLES: When?

ROGER: When I was a kid. I thought I'd be a professional adventurer.

CHARLES: I see.

ROGER: Or a rock and roll singer.
(Silence. He lets out a big sigh.)
I guess that's life.

CHARLES: I guess so.

(Silence)

(CHARLES and ROGER both stare in the distance for a long while.)

ROGER: Anyway.

(ROGER folds up CHARLES' handkerchief. He hands it to CHARLES.)

CHARLES: You can keep it.

ROGER: But it's got your initials on it.

CHARLES: I've got plenty.

ROGER: You sure?

CHARLES: Positive.
(He points his binoculars up.)

ROGER: I'm sorry.

CHARLES: What for?

ROGER: Getting so…emotional. I barely know you.

CHARLES: I don't mind.

ROGER: Technically, we know little about each other.

CHARLES: Technically. Yes.

ROGER: I didn't mean to dump my problems on you.

CHARLES: No dumping felt.

ROGER: Good.

(Silence)
Where are you from?

CHARLES: Originally?

ROGER: Yes.

CHARLES: San Francisco.

ROGER: No kidding.

CHARLES: We moved here for work. When Rebecca was a baby.

ROGER: She was born in San Francisco too?

CHARLES: Yes.

ROGER: I see. I see.
(Silence)
Do you—

CHARLES: Shall we continue? It's still early.

ROGER: Sure.
(He folds his camping chair. Puts it around his shoulder)
Charles?

CHARLES: Yes.

ROGER: Do you have any advice?

CHARLES: Pardon?

ROGER: Do, do you have any advice? For me.

CHARLES: Advice?

ROGER: Yes. I wasn't going to ask, but since you are my mentor…I thought maybe you might have—

CHARLES: Live within your means.

(Silence)

ROGER: Any other advice?

CHARLES: Did you hear me?

ROGER: Yes.

CHARLES: Is that not possible?

(*Silence*)

ROGER: I think Joyce and I are past that.

CHARLES: Are you sure?

ROGER: Well, at this point, we like nice things. We have really really good taste. It's hard to give that up.

CHARLES: Really.

ROGER: Neither of us grew up with much. So I think now we kind of, kind of take pride in, in, in—

CHARLES: In what?

ROGER: In being in style.

(CHARLES *just looks at* ROGER.)

ROGER: I know. It sounds ridiculous. But it's true. I'm being honest here—

CHARLES: Have you talked to her about it?

ROGER: No.

CHARLES: Then that's my advice.

ROGER: What?

CHARLES: Talk to your wife.

ROGER: And?

CHARLES: Tell her how you feel.

ROGER: I don't know about that.

CHARLES: Why not?

ROGER: She'll think I'm a failure.

CHARLES: Tell her failure is in "style".

ROGER: I'm serious.

CHARLES: Roger, read the papers. Watch the news. A lot of people are struggling. It's an endless recession. It's nothing to be ashamed of. It's reality.

ROGER: Do you know how terrifying it is? *Struggling?*

CHARLES: Yes.

ROGER: I mean, once you start to slip, how far down will you go?

CHARLES: Talk to your wife. Tell her you're overwhelmed. Women are much more forgiving than we give them credit for.

ROGER: I've stopped going to work.

(Silence)

CHARLES: What?

ROGER: I've…I've stopped going to work.

CHARLES: Why?

ROGER: I don't see the point anymore. I can't make enough money and adding all the numbers just seems impossible and pointless so…

CHARLES: What the hell do you do all day?

ROGER: I go to Starbucks and watch people. Or I drive around. Or I just sit in my car.

CHARLES: All day?

ROGER: Yes.

CHARLES: And do what?

ROGER: Listen to the radio. Watch birds. Cry.

CHARLES: And what do you tell your wife?

(ROGER just shakes his head.)

CHARLES: I see.
(Silence)
Oh boy.
(Silence)
Let me tell you something.

ROGER: Please.

CHARLES: I had a period once…of, of…

ROGER: What?

CHARLES: *Doubt* about my life, my path, my role as a husband, father, and I talked to my wife about it—

ROGER: What happened to you?

CHARLES: The details aren't important, but—

ROGER: The details are very important to me—

CHARLES: I talked to my wife…told her everything I felt, and you know what she said?

ROGER: What?

CHARLES: "Grow up, Charles."

ROGER: Ouch.

CHARLES: It was absolutely true.

ROGER: What happened?

CHARLES: Suffice it to say, Gail was a very smart woman. Much smarter than I. She could see what I was doing.

ROGER: What were you doing?

CHARLES: Looking for a way out.

ROGER: Of what?

CHARLES: My life. Adulthood. I wanted to stop time, go back, or run.

ROGER: You think I'm doing that?

CHARLES: What do you think?

(Silence)

(Sound of a bird O S)

CHARLES: Hear that?

ROGER: What?

CHARLES: Listen.

(Sound of bird O S)

*(*CHARLES *points his binoculars.)*

CHARLES: Brown-headed Cowbird. *Molothrus ater.*

*(*ROGER *points his binoculars.)*

ROGER: Huh.

CHARLES: The females lay their eggs in other birds' nest, and never come back. Never raise them themselves. Males get off scott-free all together.

ROGER: Seriously?

CHARLES: The host bird feeds the chicks, sometimes at the expense of her own young, while the cowbirds just move on. No responsibility, whatsoever.

ROGER: Huh.

CHARLES: They are my least favorite bird.

*(*ROGER *points his binoculars to see the bird again.)*

*(*CHARLES *and* ROGER *watch as the bird flies away.)*

ROGER: And you?

*(*CHARLES *adds the bird to his note-pad.)*

CHARLES: What about me?

ROGER: What did you do?

CHARLES: When?

ROGER: When you're wife said—

CHARLES: I grew up.

ROGER: How?

CHARLES: Oh, that's not important.

ROGER: It is to me. It is very important. I need—

CHARLES: You have to find that out for yourself.

ROGER: Is that when you started birding?

CHARLES: No.

(Silence)

ROGER: You call that advice?

CHARLES: No.

ROGER: Good, because I was really looking for something useful—

CHARLES: I don't believe in advice.

ROGER: Why not?

CHARLES: No one ever takes it.
(He begins to exit.)

ROGER: But—

CHARLES: Let's go.

(ROGER follows.)

ROGER: Charles?

CHARLES: No more talking.

ROGER: But—

CHARLES: Let us enjoy this beautiful day.

ROGER: But—

CHARLES: And the pleasure of silently looking, listening. Free from our troubles for a few hours.

ROGER: But—

CHARLES: Sshh…Roger…from here on out, we are not talking, or crying, we are quiet and listening.
(He stops. Listens)

(ROGER begins to say something. CHARLES holds up his hand to stop him. Puts his hand to his ear)

(ROGER listens.)

(The sound of bird O S)

(CHARLES *points, exits toward the sound, listening.* ROGER *puts* CHARLES' *handkerchief in his pocket, and exits after him, listening.*)

Scene 5

(Los Feliz living room)

*(*JOYCE *enters in workout gear, fresh from a run, with the mail under her arm.)*

(She exits and returns with a glass of water and looks over the room, mail still under her arm.)

(She puts down the water and walks to adjust a crocked knick-knack on a shelf. And then another. She takes down a picture of one of the boys as a baby and looks closer at it. Rubs her hand on the photo, and puts it back.)

(She scans the room and notices a pillow on the couch that needs adjusting. She puts the mail on the couch, fluffs the pillow, then decides to switch the pillow with another on a chair.)

(She stands back, scanning to see if she likes the pillow there.)

(No)

(She decides to move the chair, with the pillow, across the room to a new spot.)

(She stands back, looks, then sits in the chair. Sees how she likes the vantage point from the chair.)

(No)

(She tries the chair in another place in the room. Stands back. Looks. Sits in the chair. Scans the room. And...)

(No. No good)

(*She moves the chair back where it was in the first place. Moves the pillow back to the couch, and leaves both pillows on the couch. She stands back, tilts her head, looks. And…*)

JOYCE: Cute.

(*She sits on the couch. Moves the pillows over just a bit, a final adjustment. There.*)

(*She looks around the room.*)

(*She just sits looking. Staring at the things in her living room.*)

(ROGER *enters in suit and tie.*)

ROGER: Oh. Hi. You're home.

JOYCE: Hi, honey. You're early.

ROGER: What are you doing?

JOYCE: You think we should change the rug in here?

ROGER: No.

JOYCE: Hmm.

ROGER: Where are the boys?

JOYCE: Soccer.

(ROGER *looks at his watch.*)

ROGER: Oh. Right. I thought I'd do some work from home.

(JOYCE *begins sorting the mail. Magazine, magazine, magazine, [*New Yorker, Harpers, People—*oh—she checks to see who's on the cover—save that for later]. Catalogue, catalogue, catalogue, catalogue, catalogue.*)

JOYCE: Uh huh.
(*A letter falls out of the stack of catalogues.*)

ROGER: Hear that?
(*He makes the sound of a hummingbird flying.*)
Zzzzzhhhh.

(He glances out the window.)

*(*JOYCE *opens the letter.)*

ROGER: Hummingbird.

JOYCE: Uh huh.

ROGER: Right there. Zzzzzhhhh.

JOYCE: There's something here from the Gas Company.

ROGER: I do the bills on line.

JOYCE: Well. This is not a bill.

ROGER: What is it?

JOYCE: A disconnection notice.

ROGER: What?

*(*JOYCE *hands it to* ROGER.*)*

JOYCE: Did you pay it?

ROGER: Of course.

JOYCE: Then why are we getting a disconnection notice?

ROGER: Good question.

JOYCE: It says we have to go down there and pay, in person, if we don't want it disconnected.

ROGER: I'll go. I'll deal with it.

JOYCE: Did you pay the bill?

ROGER: Of course.

JOYCE: Then why would we get the notice?

ROGER: I have no idea. It must be a mistake. I've been busy. But I will get to the bottom of this. *(He puts the notice in his pocket.)*

JOYCE: Give it to me.

ROGER: No.

JOYCE: Give it to me and I'll go.

ROGER: No.

JOYCE: I'll call them. If you're busy—

ROGER: I'll deal with it, Joyce. It's just a big mistake. A mix-up.

JOYCE: Are you sure?

ROGER: Yes. Please. I've got it.

(ROGER *walks back to the window.* JOYCE *watches him.*)

JOYCE: Roger.

ROGER: Another hummingbird. Or the same one. Feeding on those flowers. Just having a little meal. Hey buddy.
(He watches the bird.)
I think that bird just flipped me off.

JOYCE: No he didn't.

ROGER: I'm serious. That hummingbird flipped me off. He bent his wing and… Can you believe that? I mean, ok, not literally, but the look in his eye was like he—

JOYCE: Is there something you're not telling me?

ROGER: No.

JOYCE: You're sure?

ROGER: Yes.

JOYCE: Really?

(Silence)

ROGER: Well, I guess there is one thing.

JOYCE: What?

ROGER: Well.

JOYCE: What? Don't scare me.

ROGER: I, I think I have a strange but very special relationship with birds. I think they see something in me.

(Silence)

JOYCE: No they don't.

ROGER: I know it sounds silly, but I really think, I do think they know who I am. They see who I am. The real me.

JOYCE: And who is that?

(ROGER begins to try and explain.)

ROGER: I know it's sounds…
(He gives her a good long look.)
Have I told you how beautiful you look lately?

JOYCE: Are we in trouble?

ROGER: What? You and me?

JOYCE: Financially.

ROGER: No. Geez. Please. Joyce. That was just a mistake. On *their* part. Please.

JOYCE: Really?

ROGER: Really. I'll sort it out. Can't I just compliment you?

JOYCE: I look awful right now.

ROGER: No you don't. You are so beautiful—

JOYCE: C'mon. I just went running and—

ROGER: You are beautiful, super sexy, and I love you very much.

JOYCE: Okay.

ROGER: "Okay"?

JOYCE: Thank you.
(Silence)
I appreciate that.

ROGER: Uh huh.

JOYCE: What?

(Silence)
What?

ROGER: That's it?

JOYCE: What do you want me to say?

ROGER: I'm giving you "passion" right now—

JOYCE: You are?

ROGER: You wanted me to give you more passion—

JOYCE: But what did you expect? I need to take a shower first if you want to have sex—

ROGER: You "love me too".

JOYCE: Oh. Of course. Of course I love you.

(JOYCE kisses ROGER.)

ROGER: Thank you.

(JOYCE fixes ROGER's hair.)

JOYCE: I love you very much.

ROGER: Good.

(JOYCE kisses ROGER.)

JOYCE: I've got to get in the shower before the Gas Company turns the hot water off.

ROGER: Joyce.

JOYCE: I'm kidding. I've got to hurry to pick up the boys.
(She begins to exit.)

JOYCE: Hey, you want to pick them up?

ROGER: Me?

JOYCE: Yes. Since you're home early. You can take a minute to pick them up, right?

(Silence)

ROGER: I guess. Sure. Where?

JOYCE: At soccer.

ROGER: Right.

JOYCE: It would be a big surprise for them. They'd love it.

ROGER: Sounds great. Good idea.

JOYCE: And why don't you take them to get some yogurt or something afterward? Make it special.

ROGER: Great. Will do.

JOYCE: Good. I love you, Roger.

ROGER: I love you too.

JOYCE: And please pay that gas bill.

ROGER: I did pay it—

(JOYCE exits.)

(ROGER turns his attention out the window.)

Scene 6

(Slide: A year and a half ago)

(Outside. Early morning)

(CHARLES enters, followed by REBECCA, followed by TODD, her boyfriend, and finally, ROGER.)

(They are taking a break. CHARLES takes out a bottle of water.)

(TODD breathes in the air.)

(REBECCA looks through her backpack.)

(ROGER is checking out TODD. We watch ROGER check him up and down, as TODD checks out the nature around him. [TODD is handsome, expensively dressed, and perfect.])

ROGER: That's a nice jacket.

TODD: Oh. Thank you.

ROGER: Is it Gortex?

TODD: Yes.

(ROGER *nods.* TODD *returns his attention to enjoying the nature.)*

ROGER: What do you do for a living?

TODD: Pardon?

ROGER: What do you do? For a living.

TODD: I develop software.

ROGER: Software. Really? For who?

TODD: Apple.

ROGER: Macintosh?

TODD: We call it Apple. Yes.

ROGER: I see. Interesting business.

TODD: It is.

ROGER: And you live in Los Angeles and do that? I thought they were located—

TODD: San Francisco.

ROGER: San Francisco. Lovely city.

TODD: Yes.

ROGER: So you and Rebecca have a long distance relationship.

TODD: Pretty much.

(ROGER *moves in closer.)*

ROGER: How's that working out?

TODD: Fine. Great.

ROGER: "Fine" or "great"?

TODD: Great.

(REBECCA *puts her arm around* TODD.*)*

REBECCA: You hungry, sweetheart? I brought some sandwiches.

TODD: Not yet. Thank you.

REBECCA: Roger?

ROGER: Did you make them?

REBECCA: I did.

ROGER: I'd love one. Thank you.

CHARLES: There's no meat on them.

ROGER: Really?

CHARLES: They're awful.

REBECCA: Dad.

CHARLES: It's true.

REBECCA: Dad insists on eating some kind of animal every day.

CHARLES: Survival of the fittest.

ROGER: Well, I'll take one of Rebecca's sandwiches. Made with love, I'm sure.

CHARLES: Made with tofu.

TODD: I saw a Western Kingbird in my yard last week, Charles.

CHARLES: No kidding.

TODD: I have a picture.

(REBECCA *hands* ROGER *a sandwich.*)

REBECCA: Todd is a birder.

ROGER: Really?

REBECCA: I think he knows every bird.

CHARLES: He studied.

TODD: I got into it in college. Me and my fraternity buddies.

ROGER: So you were a nerd.

(Silence)

TODD: I guess you could say that.
(He smiles.)

REBECCA: Todd does big adventure trips every year—I think he's been around the world three times already, haven't you?

TODD: Four, actually—

REBECCA: He and Dad hit off right away. Obviously.

ROGER: Is that where you met?

REBECCA: Where?

ROGER: College.

REBECCA: No.

*(*TODD *pulls a very expensive camera from his back pack.)*

ROGER: Wow.

TODD: What?

ROGER: Nice camera.

TODD: It just came on the market. It's pretty incredible.

ROGER: Can I look at it?

TODD: Sure. Sure.

*(*TODD *hands it to* ROGER.*)*

TODD: But don't drop it. Please.
(He laughs.)
Apple pays me a lot. But that's a six thousand dollar camera you're holding.

*(*ROGER *pretends to almost drop it.)*

ROGER: Whoa.

*(*TODD *gasps.)*

ROGER: Got you!

TODD: Yes you did.

CHARLES: Roger.

ROGER: What?

CHARLES: Give him back the camera.

ROGER: Why?

CHARLES: Do you have six thousand dollars?
(He stares down ROGER.*)*

*(*ROGER *stares back at him.)*

*(*ROGER *hands back the camera to* TODD.*)*

ROGER: It's very nice.

TODD: Thanks.

ROGER: And light as a feather.

*(*TODD *smiles.)*

TODD: Amazing technology. Things almost look more real on here than they do in real life.

ROGER: That's impossible.

TODD: I'm joking, of course.
(He smiles.)

REBECCA: Todd's a gadget guy.

TODD: I'm really still learning how to use it.

REBECCA: Which means he's already mastered it.

TODD: No.

REBECCA: Todd is very type A. If you haven't noticed.

TODD: I am not.

REBECCA: He runs triathlons. Volunteers at the food bank. Is a Big Brother. He makes us all look lazy and feel guilty.

TODD: I do not.

REBECCA: You do.

ROGER: I'm a big brother.

REBECCA: In the Big Brother program?

ROGER: In my family.

REBECCA: This, this is a program for disadvantaged kids—

ROGER: Oh right. Right. Of course. Ha. That. I've heard of that. Of course. Good for you.

TODD: I think it's important. To mentor. Boys need that.

ROGER: If you have time. I have kids.

TODD: How many?

ROGER: Two. Boys.

TODD: Ah. Good for you.

ROGER: I think it's important. To father. But it's a much bigger commitment than being a mentor, of course. Much bigger. Much more difficult to manage.

TODD: Of course.

ROGER: Do you have commitment issues?

CHARLES: Everyone rested up? Ready to move on?

REBECCA: Dad, this isn't a race.

CHARLES: Who said it was?

REBECCA: You push too hard lately. Everything's a rush. What's the hurry?

CHARLES: I'm here for birds, not conversation.

REBECCA: Some of us are here for both. And to relax. And enjoy each other's company.

TODD: I'm ready to keep moving, Charles.

ROGER: I haven't eaten my sandwich.

(CHARLES *looks at* ROGER.)

CHARLES: Then eat it.

(ROGER *unwraps it and takes a bite. It's awful.*)

ROGER: Wow. What else is on here?

REBECCA: Soy mayonnaise. Steamed kale. Pickled beets.

ROGER: It's very...healthy-tasting.

TODD: Rebecca is a fantastic cook.

REBECCA: I don't have much time, with work, but—

ROGER: Where'd you two meet?

(TODD *stares dreamily at* REBECCA.)

TODD: At a yoga workshop in Big Sur.

ROGER: When?

REBECCA: Last summer.

(TODD *smiles at* REBECCA.)

TODD: It was meant to be, I guess.

REBECCA: I guess so.
(*She smiles at* TODD, *blushing.*)

ROGER: So you two don't really know each other that well.

TODD: No, I'd say we know each other pretty well.

REBECCA: Me too.

ROGER: Are you sure? How many months is that—

CHARLES: Let's wind it up, folks.

REBECCA: Dad. Jesus. C'mon. Relax.

CHARLES: You relax. This is not my social hour here.

REBECCA: Why do you have to stress us all out? Seriously.

(ROGER *wraps the sandwich back up.*)

ROGER: I'm just going to save this sandwich for later. It is a treasure—

CHARLES: You are stressing *me* out, Rebecca. Come join me when you are finished flapping your jaws and flirting with your boyfriends. I'm here for the quiet and the birds.

(He quickly exits.)

REBECCA: Jesus. He's so snappy and impatient lately. Every birding trip is a rush to see as many as he can—

ROGER: You probably shouldn't have brought Todd, Rebecca.

(Silence)

No offense, Todd, but I think you are stressing Charles out.

TODD: How?

ROGER: All your expensive gear.

TODD: What?

ROGER: It's very shiny. And intimidating.

TODD: What are you talking about?

ROGER: It's not good for the birds either.

TODD: What?

ROGER: Birds like simple things. You've seen what Charles wears. And Rebecca. Earth tones. Subtle, natural clothes. Not too expensive, but tasteful and attractive. Making the birds feel relaxed and at home. Rebecca is a physical therapist. She's very aware of things like this.

REBECCA: Like what?

ROGER: Not intimidating or irritating the birds.

REBECCA: I really don't think I've ever thought about that—

TODD: That makes no sense what's so ever.

ROGER: It does if you think about it.

(TODD *smiles.*)

TODD: No. It doesn't. Not one bit.
(*He looks over* ROGER.)
What about your clothes? Those aren't cheap or—

ROGER: They are not as expensive as yours. The birds know that. They are very aware of irritating things.
(*Silence*)
Seriously.

(TODD *smiles.*)

REBECCA: Shall we catch up with, Dad? I don't want him to go too far without us.

TODD: Yes. Please. I'm ready to move on.
(*He smiles and quickly exits.*)

ROGER: Rebecca?

REBECCA: Yes, Roger.

ROGER: Are you in love with him?

REBECCA: Yes.

ROGER: Don't you find him a bit…

REBECCA: A bit what?

ROGER: Too…

REBECCA: Too what?

ROGER: Perfect?

REBECCA: No.

ROGER: He smiles too much.

REBECCA: Roger—

ROGER: And he's too sexy.

REBECCA: Roger, really—

ROGER: What's wrong with him? Where are the flaws? The weaknesses? The emotional trauma of childhood and adolescent teasing that make a man truly interesting in his adult life? That man has clearly never been teased for accidentally farting in class or his excessive acne or—

REBECCA: Roger?

ROGER: Yes?

REBECCA: Let's just move on. My dad is waiting.

(Silence)

ROGER: Of course.

(REBECCA begins to exit.)

ROGER: Rebecca?

REBECCA: What?

ROGER: It's really good to see you. I think about you all the—

REBECCA: Thanks, Roger.
(She smiles at him.)
(She exits.)

(ROGER looks at his own clothes, and follows.)

Scene 7

WOMAN'S VOICE: Orange-crowned Warbler.

(The sound of an Orange-crowned Warbler)

(Night)

(The Los Feliz home)

(ROGER alone on the couch in the living room.)

(He is listening to a recording of bird songs to learn their sounds. [Each recording has a calm WOMAN'S VOICE introducing the bird, and several sounds of the bird, about 50 seconds in length] The very calm WOMAN'S VOICE says:)

WOMAN'S VOICE: Western Bluebird.

(The sound of Western Bluebird)

(As ROGER *listens, he combs through a Peterson's Field Guide of Birds. He has a stack of birding guides beside him.)*

(He takes notes in a note book.)

*(*JOYCE *enters in her robe, rubbing night lotion on her face.)*

JOYCE: You working?

ROGER: No. Yes. Improving my bird song recognition. Listening is a huge part of the process, you know.
(He makes a note.)
I'm meeting Charles in the morning and he's asked me to be prepared for what we might see. Knowing by sight is the other big part, of course.

JOYCE: Sure.

ROGER: The details.

JOYCE: Charles has really taken you under his wing. So to speak.

ROGER: He knows a lot.

*(*JOYCE *takes a seat next to* ROGER *on the couch. She grabs one of the field guides.)*

JOYCE: So what is it about these birds.

ROGER: What do you mean?

JOYCE: Why are you so interested in them now?

ROGER: I don't know. They're beautiful. Free.

JOYCE: You said you thought they saw the real you.

WOMAN'S VOICE: California Towhee.

(The sound of a California Towhee)

JOYCE: Who would that be?

ROGER: Good question.

JOYCE: Uh huh.

(ROGER *laughs. Takes notes*)

JOYCE: Is part of the thrill just seeing them in nature?

ROGER: And recognizing what kind they are. Their song. They're mating patterns. Migration. Etc.

JOYCE: I see.

ROGER: It's hard to explain. It's a feeling, I guess.
(*He makes a other note.*)
"California Towhee."

JOYCE: Have you thought of taking the boys with you?

ROGER: No.

JOYCE: Have you thought about taking me?

ROGER: I didn't think you were interested.

JOYCE: I'm not.

ROGER: So what's the problem?

JOYCE: There's no problem. I just think it would be nice if maybe we had something together.

ROGER: We have plenty together.

JOYCE: Like what?

ROGER: Children.

JOYCE: True.
(*Silence*)
True.

WOMAN'S VOICE: Western Kingbird.

(*The sound of a Western Kingbird*)

JOYCE: Roger?

ROGER: Yes?

JOYCE: What would you think of having another baby?

ROGER: I would think that is crazy. And a terrible idea.

JOYCE: Really?

ROGER: I thought we decided two kids was exactly what we both wanted.

JOYCE: It was.

ROGER: Good.

JOYCE: But lately, lately I've been thinking that…I've been feeling like it might be nice to try for one more… if it's still possible…it may not even be possible, at my age, but, why not try…why not try…just to see—

ROGER: Do you really want to do that?

JOYCE: Maybe. Yes.

ROGER: You're just getting your own life back, aren't you?

JOYCE: Yes.

ROGER: Are you just bored?

(Silence)

JOYCE: Maybe. I don't know.

WOMAN'S VOICE: Bewick's Wren.

(The sound of a Bewick's Wren)

ROGER: Do you want to go back to work?

JOYCE: Maybe. I don't know.

(Silence)

ROGER: Joyce.

JOYCE: What?

ROGER: What do you want?

JOYCE: I don't know. Honestly. Something. I want *something*.

WOMAN'S VOICE: Western Wood-Peewee.

(The sound of a Western Wood-Peewee)

ROGER: Then think about it. Seriously. Do you really want a newborn? A tiny *newborn*? Remember how much work that was? The stinky diapers? The sleepless nights? Holding their fragile little necks and heads up all the time? It was very stressful.

JOYCE: It wasn't that bad.

ROGER: It was worse.

JOYCE: I don't remember it that way.

ROGER: Well, then you are clearly suffering from early onset Alzheimer's and that tells me that another child in your care might be a very big mistake.

JOYCE: Roger.

ROGER: I'm serious. You might put the baby in the freezer. Or put her to your ear, thinking she's the telephone.

JOYCE: You think it would be a little girl?

ROGER: No.

JOYCE: Roger. How wonderful—

ROGER: Stop.

JOYCE: It could be—

ROGER: No.

WOMAN'S VOICE: Mourning Dove.

(The sound of a Mourning Dove)

JOYCE: Can we think about it? I love the idea of thinking about a baby, imagining it, the possibility of—

ROGER: No.

JOYCE: Why not?

ROGER: We can't afford it.

JOYCE: Yes we can.

ROGER: We can't afford another child.

JOYCE: Yes we can.

ROGER: No we can't.

JOYCE: That's just an excuse.

ROGER: No it's not.

WOMAN'S VOICE: Mountain Bluebird.

(The sound of a Mountain Bluebird)

ROGER: It's not an excuse. It is not an excuse at all. It's the truth.

JOYCE: No—

ROGER: We can't afford anything else, Joyce. Nothing. Not one more thing. Nothing.

JOYCE: What are you saying?

(Silence)

ROGER: We're broke.

JOYCE: What?

ROGER: We're broke.

(Silence)

JOYCE: How broke?

ROGER: Everything.

JOYCE: But, but what about your job? Our savings? Did you get fired—

ROGER: What job? What savings?

(Silence)

JOYCE: Are you kidding with me?

ROGER: No. I'm not.

(JOYCE slaps his face. ROGER's glasses fly across the room.)

WOMAN'S VOICE: American Dipper.

(The sweet sound of an American Dipper)

(JOYCE *and* ROGER *stare at each other as the sound of the bird chirps on…)*

END OF ACT ONE

(The Los Feliz house is packed up into boxes during the intermission)

ACT TWO

Scene 1

(Slide: One year ago)

(ROGER stands among the boxes of his Los Feliz home. The couch remains, and on it, a sheet and a pillow.)

ROGER: This is really how I like best to remember this house. Not in it's heyday, full of holidays and birthday parties and loud with the kid's shouting, but as it stood in the in-between. Neither ours, nor someone else's yet. Our footprint is already fading here… Like the day the house finch family left their nest on our back porch…I had watched all but one chick leave, and then one morning it suddenly just sat there. Empty. Covered in tiny feathers, remnants of tiny pieces of egg shell, and an inch of bird poop… All the chicks had learned how to fly, one by one, and left, and I was so sad the morning I found it empty. A part of me left with that family. Will some bird bring it back to me? …And why didn't I see that final chick go? Should I have gotten up earlier? Was the little guy scared? I'm sure his parents helped him learn how to fly, but without me there to watch, did it miss my big eyes in the window, cheering him on? Or maybe they were all relieved to get the hell away from the big-eyed monster in the house, staring at them twenty-four-seven. And that cocksucker father, did he miss me? Did he wonder what would happen to me? …Did I have an impact on his house finch life,

as he did mine? …What did he see in me? And did he
hide his troubles from his wife, avoid his kids, take up
people watching, gain ten pounds, and spend a year at
Starbucks instead of the office? …Maybe… Maybe.
(He takes in the boxes, the house.)
We bought this house when Joyce was pregnant with
our first son. It was way over-priced, when the housing
market was at it's peak in Los Angeles. (Or, the last
time it was at it's peak.) I knew we were spending too
much, but it was "so perfect for us" (Joyce's words),
and "interest rates were so low" (my words), and
"we could get a great mortgage so easily" (the bank's
words) …so…like millions of others, we moved in
with big dreams to a house we couldn't afford…and
then made ourselves forget about that part as our first
son turned into a second son, and toddler toys and
primary-colored objects overtook our life…and we
called this place home.
(He lights a cigarette. Enjoys the first drag)
Home, as the house finch family taught me, is
sometimes a temporary joy you leave behind…covered
in a pile of poop.
*(He takes another drag of the cigarette. He puts on his newer
glasses [the same ones from the very first scene of the play])*
Poop and good memories.
(Silence)
But there is still this one thing, one thing that I can't—

JOYCE: *(O S)* Roger?

(ROGER quickly puts out the cigarette in a glass.)

*(He folds the sheet on the couch, and moves the pillow that
has become his new sleeping spot.)*

(JOYCE enters.)

JOYCE: I know you're smoking.

ROGER: I am not.

JOYCE: Give me one.

(ROGER *hands* JOYCE *a cigarette.*)

JOYCE: And the lighter.

(ROGER *takes the lighter from his pocket, and hands it to* JOYCE.)

JOYCE: Have you seen my purse?

ROGER: No.

JOYCE: Where are the boys?

ROGER: Outside. Zach is pushing Kyle on the swings, I think.

JOYCE: That's good. I told them I want them to enjoy this place as much as they can before we have to go.

(ROGER *gathers his birding gear from a corner of the stage.*)

JOYCE: Where are you going?

ROGER: I'm meeting Charles at the park—

JOYCE: Now?

ROGER: Yes.

JOYCE: I thought you were going to do some job hunting.

ROGER: On a Saturday?

JOYCE: Why not?

ROGER: Who is hiring on a Saturday?

JOYCE: McDonalds. Carl's Junior. Taco Bell. Starbucks. Pizza Hut. Jack in the Box. Denny's. All hire on a Saturday.

ROGER: I'll be back this afternoon.
(*He begins to exit.*)

JOYCE: I'm taking the boys to Disneyland.

ROGER: But I thought we said—

JOYCE: I am using a credit card. I don't care. I'm not going to make them suffer.

(*Silence*)

Karen invited us to go with her and her kids.

ROGER: But—

JOYCE: Since Disneyworld is out, they should at least be able to go to Disney*land*. I'm not going to tell them we can't afford to take them with their friends. And I'm certainly not telling Karen...I'll be damned if I'm telling her our problems—

(ROGER *exits.*)

(JOYCE *looks around her house.*)

(*She lights the cigarette, and takes a drag. She begins to exit, then comes back and addresses the audience.*)

JOYCE: For the record, I thought I had married *the* most dependable, trustworthy, *truthful* man I had ever met. He was trustworthy, he was interesting and very odd and funny, and I thought, "he will save me from conformity!" I mean, I knew Roger was odd. He was weird, but, you know, weird in a mostly normal package. I thought here is a man who I can build a life with, a good solid life, but with whom I will never get bored and who will keep me from growing dull and boring. I can be myself. We won't judge each other's quirks and hobbies. It will be a really interesting life together. *Our* version of the American dream. Unique. The way we wanted it to be, on our terms, our standards.

(*Silence*)

I gladly handed over the finances to him when I quit work. I wanted to raise babies.

(*Silence*)

This is our *unique* American Dream? Foreclosure? Debt? Bankruptcy?

ZACH: *(O S)* Mom?

JOYCE: What?

ZACH: *(O S)* I'm hungry.

JOYCE: There's food in the kitchen, Zach!

ZACH: *(O S)* There's nothing good left.

JOYCE: Talk to your father about that.

ZACH: *(O S)* What?
(Silence)
Where's Dad?

JOYCE: Watching birds.

ZACH: *(O S)* What?
(Silence)
Mom?

JOYCE: I'll be right there!

Scene 2

(Outside)
(ROGER enters reading his field guide, and checks his watch.)
(He waits.)
(He points his binoculars to the trees.)
(Checks his field guide)
(CHARLES finally enters.)

ROGER: You're late.

CHARLES: You're on time.

ROGER: You just missed a nice Lincoln's Sparrow.

CHARLES: Sorry to hear it.

ROGER: He smiled at me.

CHARLES: Uh huh.

ROGER: It's as if the birds know something.

CHARLES: What?

(ROGER *finally looks up from his field guide.*)

ROGER: The truth. It's terrifying.

CHARLES: Uh huh.

ROGER: You feeling okay?

CHARLES: Yes. I just missed my alarm.

ROGER: Party hard last night?

CHARLES: Uh huh.

ROGER: Seriously, what *do* you do at night?

CHARLES: What do you mean?

ROGER: What's a typical night for you? You watch tv? Read? Play bridge?

CHARLES: Why?

ROGER: I'm curious.

CHARLES: Why?

ROGER: I want to know more about you.

CHARLES: Why?

ROGER: Why not? Are you a spy?

CHARLES: If I were a spy, with international intrigue and clandestine diplomatic connections at my disposal, do you think I'd be hanging out with you?

(*Silence*)

ROGER: So you watch T V.

CHARLES: Most nights.

ROGER: Are you happy with your life?

CHARLES: What kind of question is that?

ROGER: A simple one. Are you happy?

CHARLES: That's not simple.

ROGER: Are you?

CHARLES: (Jesus.)

ROGER: Charles.

(Silence)

CHARLES: I miss my wife. No more personal questions.

ROGER: Is Rebecca coming today?

CHARLES: I knew that's where this was going—

ROGER: Is she?

CHARLES: No.

ROGER: Why not?

CHARLES: She's in San Francisco.

ROGER: Still with that guy, huh?

CHARLES: Yes.

ROGER: What's his name again?

CHARLES: Todd.

ROGER: Of course. What does she see in him?

CHARLES: Roger.

ROGER: Really. Is it the money? Because he's loaded
and is probably set for life, and has great clothes and
impeccable taste and easy to be with and socially
conscious and a perfect smile?

CHARLES: Because he's good to her.

(Silence)

ROGER: I suppose there's that.

CHARLES: Yes.

ROGER: I don't like him.

CHARLES: I don't care.

ROGER: I'm serious, Charles.

CHARLES: I'm sure you are but I don't want to hear it.

ROGER: But—

CHARLES: They're engaged.

ROGER: To be married?

CHARLES: Yes.

(Silence)

ROGER: How do you feel about that?

CHARLES: It's not about me. He makes her happy. I want her to be happy. There. She's happy, I'm happy with my life.

ROGER: Uh huh.

(Silence)

CHARLES: That's our job as fathers. To want what's best for our kids. What else can we really give them?

ROGER: I don't know anymore.

(Silence)

CHARLES: Shall we get this show on the road? The morning is passing us by.

ROGER: We've packed up the house.

CHARLES: All of it?

ROGER: Most of it. Yes. We tried to leave as much of the boy's rooms as we could.

(Silence)

CHARLES: How are they doing?

ROGER: Okay. I think. Kyle built a fort with the boxes, and he refuses to invite me inside, so…

CHARLES: Kyle's the younger one?

ROGER: Yeah. And Zach just stares at me. Blankly.

(Silence)

CHARLES: How's Joyce?

ROGER: Oh, you know…furious. She kicks me a lot.

CHARLES: Did the house sell?

ROGER: Not yet.

CHARLES: It will.

ROGER: I know but I'm hoping it won't sell too soon because it gives us more time to figure out what the hell we're going to do.

(Silence)

CHARLES: I don't envy you, Roger.

ROGER: Me either. I don't even like me.

CHARLES: How are you holding up?

ROGER: Scared.
(Silence)
Very very scared.
(Silence)
But I can't show Joyce that. Or the boys. You know?

CHARLES: Of course.
(Silence)
Do you need anything?

ROGER: A million dollars.

CHARLES: Anything else?

ROGER: A place to move my family.

CHARLES: Well—

ROGER: My pride. Manhood. A miracle. And the desire to—

CHARLES: Do you need something that I can actually help you with?

ROGER: I know you don't believe in giving advice, so I won't ask for that.

CHARLES: Good—

ROGER: So, no. I don't need anything that you can help me with. But thanks for asking.

CHARLES: I'm here for support. Any time.

ROGER: I will take that. That I could use. Thank you.

(Silence)

CHARLES: Okay then…
(Silence)
Shall we watch some birds?

ROGER: Please.

(CHARLES points his binoculars up. Points to a bird)

(ROGER puts his binoculars to the sky.)

(They stand looking and listening.)

ROGER: Charles?

CHARLES: Sshh.

(Silence)

ROGER: I love you, buddy.

CHARLES: Okay now. Let's not be ridiculous.

Scene 3

(Slide: Six months ago. Studio City, CA)

(The same couch from the Los Feliz home, sits in the middle of the stage. It is the center piece of ROGER and JOYCE's two-bedroom apartment in Studio City.)

(ROGER sleeps on the couch.)

(JOYCE enters in a nice dress and heels, putting on her earring. She kicks the couch with her heel.)

JOYCE: Get up, Roger.

ROGER: What?

JOYCE: Get up. I've got to be at work in half an hour. And I need you to drop the kids off at school.

ROGER: Okay. Okay.
(He sleepily rises out of bed.)
Did they eat yet?

JOYCE: They're in the kitchen eating now.

ROGER: Okay. Good. Good.

JOYCE: And you'll pick them up, right?

ROGER: Right.

JOYCE: Good. Thanks.
(She puts on some lipstick.)

JOYCE: How do I look?

ROGER: Great.

JOYCE: Really? You think this dress is too tight?

ROGER: No.

JOYCE: I'm meeting with a new marketing team, and I don't want to look too sexy, but I don't want to look too stiff either.

ROGER: I'd say that was perfect.

JOYCE: Perfect to sell high sugar high caffeine energy drinks?

ROGER: Pretty much.

JOYCE: Good.

(A cell phone ring)

JOYCE: Is that your phone or mine?

ROGER: I don't know. Mine, I think.

(JOYCE grabs her purse and checks.)

JOYCE: It's yours. Shit, I'm late. I gotta go. Bye boys!
(She waits.)

JOYCE: I said, bye boys!

KYLE & ZACH: *(O S)* Bye, Mom!

JOYCE: Listen to your father!

ZACH: *(O S)* Why?

ROGER: Hey!

JOYCE: Because I said so! You hear me!

KYLE & ZACH: *(O S)* Okay.

JOYCE: And don't forget your lunch!
(Silence)
Did you hear me? Zach, Kyle?

KYLE & ZACH: *(O S)* Yes.

ZACH: *(O S)* I don't want peanut butter again!

JOYCE: Too bad! That's what you're having!

ZACH: *(O S)* Mom—

JOYCE: Zach, don't start!
(She fixes her hair.)
(To ROGER*)*
Don't let them forget their lunch. Do you have cash?
For the day?

ROGER: Do you know where my phone is?

JOYCE: I don't know, Roger. Sounds like it was coming
from the couch.

*(*ROGER *checks the couch cushions.)*

JOYCE: Do you need cash?

*(*ROGER *looks underneath the couch.)*

JOYCE: Just let it go to voice mail. Do you want me to
leave you some cash?

ROGER: Well, I need to find it.
(He bends down and reaches under the couch, his face disappearing in the search.)
I think I see it. No, that's not it—

JOYCE: Roger?

ROGER: What? I'm looking for my phone…

JOYCE: I'll see you later.
(She exits.)

(ROGER finally finds his phone. He stands up and looks at the number. He puts it to his ear to hear the message.)

ZACH: *(O S)* Dad?

(ROGER is listening to the message.)

ZACH: *(O S)* Dad?

ROGER: Yeah?

ZACH: *(O S)* Where's our stupid lunch?

ROGER: Just a second!

ZACH: *(O S)* Dad? Mom said—

ROGER: I'm be right there, Zach!

ZACH: *(O S)* You don't have to yell!

(ROGER takes the phone from his ear.)

ROGER: I'm not yelling!

ZACH: *(O S)* Sounds like yelling to me!

KYLE: *(O S)* Me too!

ROGER: Don't be so damn sensitive! Jesus!
(He puts the phone down, and begins to get dressed.)

ZACH: *(O S)* Dad, Kyle's crying!

Scene 4

(A hospital waiting room)
(REBECCA sits alone in a chair.)
(ROGER enters in a hurry.)

ROGER: I'm sorry I couldn't get here earlier, but I had to take my kids to school, and my car was out of gas and—

REBECCA: No problem.

(ROGER sits down beside REBECCA.)

ROGER: How's he doing?

REBECCA: He's still in surgery.

ROGER: What have they told you?

REBECCA: It doesn't look good.
(She is trying to keep it together.)

ROGER: I'm sorry.

REBECCA: I have his phone, and I saw your name and number, and I really have no idea why I called you, I don't, but I just thought…I don't know…I thought you'd want to know and I just didn't feel like calling my other friends, and I'm really not thinking straight right now—

ROGER: I'm glad you did—

REBECCA: Todd is trying to get a flight down as soon as he can.

ROGER: I'm glad you called me.

(Silence)

REBECCA: You got new glasses.

ROGER: Oh. Yeah. My others got—

REBECCA: Nice.
(Silence)

I don't know if I can go through this again, Roger. I mean, I feel like I just went through this with my mom, and if my dad dies, then I don't know…I think I might just die too.

ROGER: No you won't.

REBECCA: I think I might.

ROGER: It might feel like you're dying, but you won't. I felt that way when I lost my parents.

REBECCA: You lost your parents?

ROGER: My mom died when I was in my twenties, then I lost my dad three years ago…I thought I would just shrivel up it hurt so much. I felt so…I don't know… ungrounded. I felt like I barely knew him, and he was gone. But you will be ok. I promise. You will.

REBECCA: I don't know.
(She starts to cry.)
I don't think I'll make it without my dad.

(ROGER digs through his pockets. He finds the handkerchief that CHARLES had given him, and hands it to REBECCA.)

(She begins to use it, then looks at it closer.)

REBECCA: Is this—

ROGER: It's clean. I washed it.

(This familiar object pretty much destroys REBECCA.)

ROGER: He lent it to me once. Told me to keep it.

(REBECCA hides her face in it.)

(ROGER puts his arm around her.)

ROGER: I'm so sorry, Rebecca. I'm so sorry.
(Silence)
We have to think positive. We have to think very positive thoughts, for your Dad. Right?

(REBECCA tries to nod.)

ROGER: A lot of people survive heart attacks. And Charles is a pretty tough guy. He's strong. He could out-walk me for days.

(REBECCA *nods.*)

ROGER: I know he would want us to sit here and be strong and quiet and not get too worried and afraid. He would want us to just sit here and listen, right?
(Silence)
Right?

REBECCA: Probably.

ROGER: So let's do that. Let's just sit here and listen and be strong and quiet for your Dad.
(Silence)
We're not afraid, Charles. We're going to be strong and sit here quietly, just like you'd want us to.

(ROGER *keeps his arm around* REBECCA *as they sit quietly.*)

ROGER: *(Quietly)* We're not afraid. We'll sit here and listen, just for you.

(ROGER *and* REBECCA *sit listening.*)

Scene 5

(Outside)

(JOYCE *on the phone.*)

JOYCE: Uh huh…uh huh…uh huh… Uh huh… Well, what did Zach do? …Did the other kid apologize—… that doesn't sound much like an apology… My husband *is* currently unemployed, but what is it that kid's business? …The truth isn't the point, it's the teasing, isn't it? I think so… This is public school, in a shitty neighborhood, a lot of kids' parents are out of work, so why was this kid picking on Zach? …I'm sorry I called it shitty, I'm, I'm sorry, I didn't mean

that... You still haven't told me what Zach said that is
so awful, and I just got home and—
(She takes a drag of the cigarette, listening.)
Is the kid an asshole?...it does seem to be the point...
Zach was probably speaking the truth, right? ...
Between you and me, Miss Baker, c'mon, you can
be honest... Okay, okay...I understand...okay... Uh
huh... Uh huh...

*(ROGER enters with a bag of garbage, at the corner of the
stage, and listens.)*

JOYCE: I, I appreciate your concern...I do...thank you...
yes, we've, we've gone through some big changes
in our family in the last year and the move and new
school has been hard on our sons, so...so...so we are
working through it, the best we can...right...right...it
is hard...yeah, uh huh, exactly...well, frankly, if Zach
wants to call his father an asshole, he's free to... In fact,
I would encourage him...I'm kidding, Miss Baker...
Okay... Uh huh...uh huh...sure...well, I've got to go.
Thanks, thanks for calling. Uh huh... Thanks again,
Miss Baker, we'll talk to Zach... Uh huh.
*(She puts the phone away, and stands thinking for a
moment. She lights a cigarette.)*

(ROGER moves in closer.)

ROGER: Hi.

JOYCE: Oh. Hi.

ROGER: Who was that?

JOYCE: Miss Baker.

ROGER: Zach's teacher?

JOYCE: Yes.

ROGER: Everything okay?

JOYCE: Zach won't apologize. For calling some kid a
name.

ROGER: What?

JOYCE: Did you tell Zach you were sorry?

ROGER: What?

JOYCE: Did you tell Zach and Kyle you were sorry, for what happened? Did you talk to the boys about it?

ROGER: I think so.

JOYCE: You *think* so?

ROGER: I think I did—

JOYCE: Tell them again. Apologize. I think they need you to hear it from you.

ROGER: Okay.

JOYCE: Try to explain it.

ROGER: Okay. But it's not so easy. I mean—

JOYCE: Why didn't you tell me, Roger? Seriously. All those months and months. Why didn't you talk to me—

ROGER: I couldn't.

JOYCE: Why?

ROGER: I didn't know how.
(Silence)
Why didn't you ever look at our accounts?

JOYCE: Don't you dare. Blame me.

ROGER: I'm not. I just—

JOYCE: Stop.
(Silence)

ROGER: You coming inside?

JOYCE: In a minute.

ROGER: I made dinner.

JOYCE: I'll be right there.

ROGER: Good day at work?

JOYCE: Yes. Busy.

ROGER: You—

JOYCE: I'm just tired.

(Silence)

ROGER: I'm sorry, Joyce.
(He exits with the garbage.)

(JOYCE takes a breath. And stays smoking)

(She takes off her high heels, hurting her feet.)

Scene 6

(A flock of birds moves overhead. Sounds of birds O S)

(ROGER enters in his birding gear.)

(The birds pass. It grows quiet.)

ROGER: We spread Charles' ashes among some of
his favorite pine trees in the Angeles forest, where
he could listen and look for his favorite birds into
eternity...It was just a few of us that day...a few
professors from Charles' school, two of Rebecca's
friends, a sister of Charles that I never knew he had...
and of course, Rebecca and what's his face...who,
in my opinion, could have given Rebecca a little bit
more affection...*Todd*, as I guess he is called, was so
preoccupied with that damn million dollar camera
and capturing the event for posterity, that Rebecca's
hand went unheld way too much of the day...I tried
to hold it once or twice, but apparently, my hand was
not what she needed in her moment of grief...I settled
for carrying her back pack...which smelled a lot like
lavender...like her hair...

(Silence)

I said my own good-bye to Charles privately…two
weeks later I went back to the same spot and cried…
cried and cried… There was so much I didn't know, so
much more I wanted to learn from him. Just like my
own father…All those feelings of, of just missing out
on the man himself…longing to know him better…
longing to understand his silence and dreams…I was
flooded and…and you know what? You know what?…
As I was standing there, crying and thinking my
own thoughts, guess who came and sat down on his
grave site? A Cooper's Hawk. A Cooper's Hawk just
sat down there, and took a little a rest…."Majestic."
"Proud"…. When I got closer, I swear the bird had
tears in his eyes too, and we looked at each other, and
he flew off…way up into the sky…and did an amazing
glide, and then off higher he went…higher…so I
waved…

(He waves to the sky.)

I waved at him…I waved until I couldn't see him
anymore…and finally I shouted…"I miss you
Charles…I miss you buddy…You were a great father
and mentor and friend… Fly on… Fly on good man…
Fly on."

(Silence)

Then I realized it was actually a *Red*-Tailed Hawk…
but, you know…I'm sure Charles understood…it was a
beautiful bird…

(He looks around.)

Now…

(He is listening.)

Now if I listen.

(He listens.)

Really listen. Every time I'm outside. And quiet.

*(Sound of many types of birds O S. [We all listen together,
as an audience. The sound of the birds grow louder and
louder.])*

ROGER: I hear the greatest symphony of Los Angeles. I hear the voices and songs that surround us every day. I hear the "true wonder" Charles taught me to hear.

(ROGER *listens. [We listen.]*)

ROGER: What might the birds be saying if we knew their language?

(*We listen.*)

ROGER: "Good morning?"

(*We listen.*)

ROGER: "Fear not?".

(*We listen.*)

ROGER: "I'm over here, darling?"

(*We listen.*)

ROGER: "Dinner at six. Cocktails at five-thirty. My nest?"

(*We listen.*)

(ROGER *grabs his binoculars.*)

ROGER: Are the birds watching us too? What are they trying to say?
(*He puts his binoculars to his eyes.*)

(*We listen.*)

ROGER: "I see who you are?"
(*He lets the binoculars down.*)
"I know what's in your heart."

(*We listen.*)

ROGER: "I know your secret."

(*We listen.*)

ROGER: "I *know.*"

(*The birds continue O S.*)

Scene 7

(The Studio City apartment)

(Night)

(JOYCE and ROGER sit side by side on the couch, watching television.)

(ROGER puts his hand on JOYCE's knee.)

(JOYCE looks at his hand.)

(Continues to watch television.)

(He moves his hand up her thigh.)

(She grabs his hand.)

JOYCE: Roger.

ROGER: Yes.

JOYCE: We talked about this.

ROGER: A long time ago. Hasn't enough time passed, and—

JOYCE: I still don't think you fully realize exactly what you did.

ROGER: Yes I do.

JOYCE: I think you have a very selective memory.

ROGER: Well, okay, that part is true, I am a bit guilty of that, but I do remember what I did—

JOYCE: What did you do?

ROGER: Joyce.

JOYCE: I'm serious.

(Silence)

ROGER: I got overwhelmed.

JOYCE: That's one way to put it. And?

(Silence)

ROGER: Stopped going to work.

JOYCE: And?

ROGER: Spent all our money.

JOYCE: And?

ROGER: Didn't tell you.

JOYCE: And?

ROGER: That's it.

JOYCE: And?

ROGER: And what?

JOYCE: Roger.

(Silence)

ROGER: Oh, and lied about it.

JOYCE: Right. For how long?

ROGER: About a year.

JOYCE: Yes. About a year.

ROGER: I do forget that part sometimes.

JOYCE: I don't.

(ROGER takes his hand off JOYCE's thigh.)

JOYCE: I still have not figured out how an accountant, an accountant, of all things, doesn't understand how to manage his money.

ROGER: We were spending way more than I made. That's simple math, Joyce.

JOYCE: You would think.

(JOYCE and ROGER watch T V for a moment.)

JOYCE: You're lucky I didn't divorce you.

ROGER: That's true.

(Silence)

JOYCE: Not that it doesn't cross my mind.

ROGER: I do remember you mentioning that. Several times.

(JOYCE *and* ROGER *watch a bit more T V.*)

ROGER: Why haven't you?

JOYCE: Divorced you?

ROGER: Yes.

JOYCE: Good question.
(Silence)
Very good question.
(Silence)

ROGER: Is it your undying love for me?

JOYCE: No.

ROGER: Is it the boys? Wanting to keep the family together?

JOYCE: No.

ROGER: Wanting to make sure they have a father?

JOYCE: No.

ROGER: No? Why not?

JOYCE: You haven't been a good father, Roger.

ROGER: That's not fair.

JOYCE: Have you?

(ROGER *turns off the T V.*)

ROGER: I'm a fun father. I think they would call me a "fun" father.

JOYCE: That's what you would like to call yourself.
(Silence)
I don't think moving out of the only home they've ever known and going to new schools and leaving their friends is what the boys would call fun.

ROGER: Do you really think I'm a bad father?

JOYCE: Most of the time, yes.

ROGER: Really?

JOYCE: Yes.

ROGER: How?

JOYCE: They barely know who you are.

ROGER: Really?

JOYCE: Yes.

(Silence)

ROGER: Really?

JOYCE: Yes.

(Silence)

ROGER: So do you want a divorce now, is that what you're telling me?

JOYCE: No.

ROGER: No?

JOYCE: No.

ROGER: Then can we please have sex? In the bed? I'm tired of sleeping on the couch. Will please you let me come sleep in the bed, with you—

JOYCE: No. Not right now.

ROGER: When?

JOYCE: I don't know.

ROGER: It's been forever.

JOYCE: Well. I'm sorry.

ROGER: So what has kept you with me? Seriously, Joyce. If I'm so awful, why have you stayed?

(Silence)

JOYCE: Sympathy.

ROGER: Sympathy?

JOYCE: Yes.

ROGER: Really? For what? My back is killing me from this couch, and you don't seem to care—

JOYCE: You have a couch to sleep on, don't you?
(Silence)
And I am still here. I'm still here, Roger. Aren't I?

ROGER: Yes.

JOYCE: You know why?

ROGER: Sympathy. You just told me.

(Silence)

JOYCE: I've learned a lot in the last year or so. I've learned a whole lot. I see things very differently now.

ROGER: Well. Me too.

JOYCE: It doesn't mean I'm not still mad at you, on every level, for making me see these new things.

ROGER: Okay.

JOYCE: But, I do have sympathy for you and all the pressure we put on you in our family. I have found great sympathy for that, and I take responsibility for being blind to how much pressure it was to keep up that big house and the schools and the organic food and the soccer camp and my facials and—

ROGER: Those were way overpriced. If you ask me.

JOYCE: That's not my point.
(Silence)
When I asked you if it was ok if I stopped working to stay home to raise the boys, I never really thought about how much responsibility that would put on you…I just thought you were fine with it, and you'd find a way to make more money. That's it. You'd take care of it. Like my dad did. You'd just make more

money. And everyone in our neighborhood made so much money, I never questioned if we were struggling. It never crossed my mind. Can you believe that?

ROGER: No.

JOYCE: I worried about it, in *theory*, but it didn't cross my *rational* mind… My *realistic* mind, wouldn't entertain the idea… And you never talked about it… and I just looked around, and on the outside, we looked just like everyone else. And that's exactly the way I wanted it. I wanted to have exactly what everyone else had. Even if it meant not seeing that we could possibly be living a lie. That your pay check couldn't cover what I saw. I wanted the possibility to do whatever I wanted, when I wanted.
(Silence)
My father had a heart-attack at forty-five.

ROGER: He did?

JOYCE: It was mild, but…

ROGER: Shit.

JOYCE: Maybe that's the big lesson of middle age.

ROGER: Surviving death?

JOYCE: That there are some things that just aren't possible anymore. That there's not enough money or time or opportunity to do everything you want.

ROGER: How sad.

JOYCE: Yeah, it sucks. But it's true.
(Silence)
I have sympathy for you because I was right there with you, blind and hungry for more. I didn't want to know how much was in our bank account. I didn't want to see that we weren't rich, young and carefree, and I didn't want to consider that maybe part of being at *this* stage in our lives, was to appreciate what we had, and

what was really was possible…and learn to accept that as just life, real adult life, not failure.

ROGER: So what you're saying is that you are actually very thankful for what I did.

JOYCE: No. I still think you're a mother fucker.

ROGER: Oh.

JOYCE: But I do understand some of it. I want to be responsible for my part. And I am trying to be supportive. *(Silence)* I'm trying. Very hard.

(Silence)

ROGER: I love you, Joyce.
(He grabs her hand and kisses it.)
More than ever.
(Silence. He kisses her arm.) So…shall we…you know… go to the bedroom…

JOYCE: No.

ROGER: C'mon, Joyce.

JOYCE: Not now.

ROGER: When?

JOYCE: When you finally get a job.

Scene 8

(Outside)

(The Burbank Airport parking lot.)

(The sounds of airplanes O S)

(REBECCA and TODD stand with their luggage. Waiting)

(TODD checks his watch.)

(REBECCA and TODD look toward the sound of a bus pulling up, and idling O S.)

(ROGER *enters in his Burbank Parking Lot, Inc. uniform and hat. He is looking up at the sky. Looking at a bird)*

(He takes a note pad from his pocket and writes it down.)

ROGER: "Rufous-Crowned Sparrow. Burbank Airport."
(He checks his watch.)
"Twelve o'five."
(He puts the note pad away, and looks straight to the luggage.)
Good morning. Good morning. Thank you for waiting.
(He finally looks up at the owners of the luggage.)
Where you folks going today?

TODD: San Francisco—

ROGER: Rebecca. It's me, Roger.

REBECCA: Oh my gosh. I'm sorry. Roger. Of course. I didn't recognize you when you got out of the bus. In the uniform. And the hat.

ROGER: It's me.

REBECCA: How are you?

ROGER: Good. Good.

REBECCA: So you work here now?

ROGER: I do.

REBECCA: Wow.

ROGER: Yeah. I meet lots of interesting people.

REBECCA: Sure sure.

ROGER: Hello, uh…uh—

TODD: Todd.

ROGER: Right.

TODD: New job, huh?

ROGER: Yep. No desk. No computer. No numbers. Fresh air. It's perfect. I love it.

TODD: Good. Good. Glad to hear it—

ROGER: Took me awhile to find it though. It's rough out there.

TODD: I know.

ROGER: I hear that Apple stock went down recently. You scared?

TODD: No.

REBECCA: Please. Todd is a wiz with money.

TODD: It's just simple math.

ROGER: Nothing is simple. Trust me.

TODD: It is if you understand it. And plan for it, and—

ROGER: I was like you once.

TODD: No you weren't.

ROGER: I was.

TODD: No. I don't think so.

ROGER: I was.

TODD: No.

ROGER: I was.

TODD: No. Roger. It is really not possible, that you have ever been like me.

ROGER: But it is.

(TODD *smiles.*)

TODD: No.

ROGER: Look at you. You've got the world at your feet. A great job, a lot of money, the perfect girl, and the wardrobe to match. Take it from me, all that could change. All of it. In an instant. And you're not even sure how. I've been there.

TODD: You think because you see me wear these clothes, you know something about me? I could care less about any of this stuff.

ROGER: Really?

TODD: It's means nothing.

ROGER: Nothing?

TODD: Yes.

ROGER: Then why spend so much money?

TODD: I work hard. I like good quality.

ROGER: I find that hard to believe.

REBECCA: Every four years Todd gives away all of his possessions.

ROGER: No.

REBECCA: Yes.

ROGER: Are you a real person? Seriously? Where did you come from?

TODD: Houston.

REBECCA: It's true.

ROGER: But *everything*? Everything you own?

TODD: Everything.

ROGER: Why?

TODD: I don't want anything to own me.

(Silence)

ROGER: Does that work?

TODD: Not always.

(Silence)

ROGER: Well. I do apologize.

TODD: No problem.

ROGER: So…can I, can I have that fancy camera, next time you're giving things away?

TODD: Sure.

ROGER: Where are you guys off to?

TODD: We're going home.

ROGER: *(To* REBECCA*)* You moved to San Francisco?

REBECCA: I did. We got married.

ROGER: Congratulations.

REBECCA: Thank you. I've been commuting back and forth to settle things with my dad's house.

ROGER: I see.

REBECCA: Yeah.

ROGER: You look fantastic. The Bay Area must agree with you.

REBECCA: It does.

ROGER: Well, you were born there, right? So—

REBECCA: How'd you know that?

ROGER: Your dad told me.

REBECCA: Actually, I wasn't born there.

ROGER: Really?

REBECCA: I was abandoned in Bakersfield as a newborn and taken to San Francisco, where my parents adopted me. Dad never told people that part.

ROGER: Wow.

TODD: You really don't need to explain everything to him—

REBECCA: Why not? It's the truth.

TODD: Of course. But it's personal, and—

ROGER: I'm almost family.

(To REBECCA*)*
Right?

TODD: Well. We should really get going. Our flight. Sweetheart.

ROGER: I bet that's why he never liked cowbirds.

REBECCA: Why?

ROGER: They abandon their eggs.

REBECCA: That's right. That's right. Yes. Maybe.

TODD: We should get going, Rebecca. Our flight leaves in forty-five minutes and—

ROGER: Your father was an interesting man.

REBECCA: Yes.

TODD: He was great.

ROGER: He—

TODD: I'm sorry, but I am really worried about the time, Roger. If we miss this flight, we can't—

ROGER: Of course. Of course.

TODD: And there are other people waiting down there in the lot. For the bus.

ROGER: Ah yes. Of course. Duty calls.

REBECCA: It's so great to see you. Are you still birding?

ROGER: Oh yes. Yes. As much as I can. With my new work schedule.

REBECCA: Right.

ROGER: I owe a lot to your dad.

REBECCA: Me too.

ROGER: I miss him.

REBECCA: Me too.

ROGER: My whole life has changed, and--it's just great to see you. You just look fantastic. You really do. I'm sure you're Dad is very proud of you, Rebecca.

REBECCA: Thank you.

TODD: Roger—

ROGER: Well. You just look—

REBECCA: I know he really appreciated your companionship. You won him over.

ROGER: It was my pleasure. My pleasure.

(REBECCA *quickly gives* ROGER *a big strong hug.*)

TODD: I hate to be a broken record, and I don't want to be rude, really, but we really should get going, Rebecca. The next flight is full.

(REBECCA *finally let's go of* ROGER.)

REBECCA: Yes. Yes. Of course.

ROGER: I'll just, I'll just get your bags.

TODD: Thanks.

REBECCA: You don't have to do that—

ROGER: It's my job. Please. I'm happy to.

REBECCA: No—

TODD: Let him.
(*He smiles at* ROGER.)
Thank you.

ROGER: I'm happy to.
(*He grabs their luggage and exits.*)

TODD: Okay then. Ready?

(REBECCA *watches* ROGER.)

TODD: Sweetheart?

REBECCA: Yes. Yes. Of course.

(REBECCA *and* TODD *follow* ROGER, *and exit.*)
(*Sound of birds O S*)

Scene 9

(*The sound of boys shouting O S*)
(*Slide: Now*)
(*Outside*)
(ROGER *enters in birding gear, and carrying two small jackets.*)

ROGER: Sshh! Quiet! Quiet up there, Zach. Sshh!
(*He watches them in the distance.*)
Kyle, don't throw that at your brother! Put the stick down!
(*He watches.*)
Put the stick down, Kyle! I said put it down, don't throw it... And wait there. I want you both to wait right there and see if you can see five birds each on the list I gave you.

KYLE & ZACH: (*O S*) Dad...c'mon!

ROGER: Whoever gets the first five birds on their list *first*, gets to pick where we go to lunch.

KYLE: (*O S*) Really?

ROGER: Yes, but you've got to look. Look hard and be quiet.

ZACH (*O S*) But, Dad. It's too early. I'm tired—

ROGER: Ssshh! You're not looking.
(*He watches them.*)
Look up, Kyle.
(*He finally turns his attention to the audience.*)
This is a nightmare. It's like birding with coyotes.
(*He looks in the distance, toward the boys.*)

I can't blame the birds for taking off as fast as they can…I often think of running the other way, and leaving them here…but, I have found a very important thing for these two boys: competition. The minute I make this a competition, they will do anything. I mean, anything. They always want to beat each other at everything, and beat everyone… They are very competitive. They want to be the best, the fastest, the tallest, the smartest, the richest…I don't know where they get that…

(He looks their way again. He puts his finger to his lip to keep them quiet, and points to the sky, the trees for them to look.)

But there is one thing in the past two years that I still haven't found…I just can't seem to find it, and I can't tell Joyce… It is my secret…maybe that house finch cocksucker took it right off my porch…maybe he has it, tucked under his wing, like a little newspaper, or inside his beak somewhere and I will never see it again… Maybe that's for the best, who knows…but I cannot for the life of me seem to find my desire to make money… It's gone…I have lost it, altogether…I have no drive, no instinct, no umph, no inclination, no desire what's so ever, to make money…None….at all…and believe me, that is a big problem…it is a big problem for my family, but a bigger problem in this country, in this world, in the universe that I currently find myself… A very big problem…I'm telling you, I am lost…missing that piece of me, that money piece, I am a man and father adrift…who am I now? What use am I? I am like a cat who's been declawed and set free in the wild…I mean it, and not to be too dramatic, but it's like trying to survive without my soul here… seriously…and yet, yet, I am telling you, my *real* soul, that part that doesn't give a shit about money, has never been more free and peaceful and calm and—

(He catches sight of the boys off stage, and shouts.)
Damn it, Zach! Do not throw rocks at the goddamn
birds. I mean it! Stop it! Kyle has already seen two
birds more than you—

ZACH *(O S)* Dad—

ROGER: Sshh! I mean it! Start looking!
*(He watches him, gives him a stern warning with his finger,
a point to the sky, and finally returns his attention to the
audience.)*
So…here I stand…a man without a drive for money
I once found at the center of my life…and now at the
center, instead, is a love of birds…our most ancient
creatures of flight, who, if you happen to find the
moment to look eye to eye, will show you the truth
about yourself. Whether you want it or not. Not a great
exchange, as Joyce might say, not a great exchange at
all…but strangely, it has brought me closer to her, and
it has brought me out here with my sons…I am trying
to be a better father…I am learning to let them know
who I am…I am learning…and I am happier…I am
trying to find a new way…
(He quickly looks to check on his sons in the distance.)
So, to that cocksucker House Finch…I say, thank you…
and fly on, good man, fly on…take my desire for
money in your beak…build a good nest with it…raise
your kids…and leave it as soon as you can…
(He walks to join his sons.)
Okay boys. Who's got the most birds?
(He claps his hands together, and exits.)

END OF PLAY